IMAGES
of America

SUNSET HILLS

Sandie Grassino for the
Sunset Hills Historical Society

ARCADIA
PUBLISHING

Published by Arcadia Publishing
Charleston, South Carolina

Library of Congress Control Number: 2009943862

For all general information, please contact Arcadia Publishing:
Telephone 843-853-2070
Fax 843-853-0044
E-mail sales@arcadiapublishing.com
For customer service and orders:
Toll-Free 1-888-313-2665

Visit us on the Internet at www.arcadiapublishing.com

This book is dedicated to Joyce Franklin, the driving force behind so many projects and so much goodwill in all areas of our lives. (Courtesy of Danielle Mohrmann.)

CONTENTS

ACKNOWLEDGMENTS

Special thanks to Jill Arnone, Susan Bennet, Pat Bessinger, Lynda S. Burge, Leslie Vander Meulen Canavan, Beth Cross and the Lindbergh School District, Eileen Dreyer, the City of Sunset Hills, Joyce Franklin, Amy Grassino, Joseph J. Grassino, Judy Guglielemencci, Jane Hake and her students, Jim Healey and Sunset Country Club, Tim Heutel and Sunset Automotive, June Jaeger, Kedrick Kennerly and the Kennerly Family Archives, Barbara Knotts, Marc Kollbaum and the St. Louis County Department of Parks and Recreation, Laura Kopp, Della Lang, the Library of Congress (LOC), Jeannie Lin, Debbie Loeffelman and Johnny's Market, Long Elementary School, John Maurath, Shelly Minnella, Danielle Mohrmann, Trish Moore, Wayne and Jeanette Ortmann, Tina Other, Tom Pearson, the St. Louis Public Library, Ann Portell Schmitz, Sunset Hills Historical Society (SHHS), Butch and Linda Thomas, the Harry S. Truman Presidential Library, Randy Wilke, Bob and Wanda Winter, and Mike Venso and Laumeier Sculpture Park.

Special thanks, also, to my wonderful editorial family at Arcadia.

INTRODUCTION

Sunset Hills is, against the background of history, a relatively new place. It was incorporated as a city in 1957, making it one of the newer cities in the St. Louis area. Perceived by many as a bedroom community of the larger metropolitan area, Sunset Hills actually has a rich history of its own. Sunset Hills represents a broad scope of the population; from starter houses to mansions, the city has them all.

Researching the history of Sunset Hills is quite challenging. Over the course of the last three centuries, the name has changed frequently. In records, it is known as Bonhomme, Carondelet, Kirkwood, Sappington, Fenton, Meramec Settlement, Gravois Settlement, St. Louis County, and possibly Heutelville. Despite its many names, the area has been a constant home for many families, some of which now include seventh-generation residents of the area.

Its rich history extends back to prehistoric tribes, as many artifacts have been found in the area's various creeks and streams and along the banks of Meramec River. Fenton, across the river from the modern Sunset Hills, is thought to have been built on top of a prehistoric Indian settlement. Mound builders also inhabited the area and remnants of their existence are still visible in the communities. Several mounds were unearthed during the excavation for several area strip malls.

According to the Indian History section of the 2006 Sunset Hills history pamphlet, the following tribes are believed to have lived in the area: Missouri, Delaware, Shawnee, Sauk and Fox (also called Renard), Miami, Chickasaw, Pottawatomie, Winnebago, Onondaga, Illinois, Peoria, Pawnee, Kickapoo, Kooncek, Cherokee, Dakotah, Padukah, and Ohio. It is believed that Chief Black Hawk of the Sauk and Fox tribes visited the area. Area legend also says that Pyesa, Black Hawk's father, was killed in the area when his tribe raided a Cherokee camp at the bend of the Meramec River.

An area in the Meramec River Valley near Minnie HaHa Beach was the site of an important trading post. Jacques Clamorgan (about 1734–1814), who was of mixed descent, reportedly including Spanish, Portuguese, African, and Welsh heritage, organized the Missouri Company for fur trade and exploration in 1794. The company was chartered by the country of Spain, which chose Clamorgan as the only white man allowed to deal directly with the Indian tribes in the area, so all bargaining for goods between the parties was brokered through him. After some partners left the Missouri Company in 1796, Clamorgan renamed the company Clamorgan, Loisel & Company. Because of these companies and his allegiance with Spain, Clamorgan was awarded land grants totaling nearly one million acres throughout Upper Louisiana. He also bought one of the largest salt works in the area, in modern-day Fenton, in 1791.

The Spanish gave many land grants in the area in the late 18th century. Besides Clamorgan, others receiving grants included Phillip Baccene, John Boli, William Boli, Gabriel Cerre, Peter Didier, Francois Lacombe, Jay Neybour, Father Peilievre, Baptiste Riviere, Sophia Shafer, John Watkins, and Conrad Wheat. John Boli ran several commercial ferries across the Meramec River, which allowed for expansion into areas west of St. Louis City. The land grants were substantial, with William Boli (under the name Sophia Shafer) receiving 340 acres, John Boli receiving 136 acres, and John Sappington receiving 126 acres.

Today, Sunset Hills encompasses 9.5 square miles and boasts more than 8,000 residents in more than 3,000 households. No longer considered just a bedroom community for St. Louis, the area is carving out its own present and future.

Many memories of Sunset Hills have been lost due to the lack of photographs. For instance, in the late 1950s and early 1960s, Ike and Tina Turner performed at the Sunset Pool, on the corner of Gravois and Sappington Barracks Roads, on weekend evenings. No usable photographs were located for the Mill Hill Fathers on Gravois Road at Hadley Hill Road. It was a beautiful place with stables and a grotto. A park used to be on Gravois Road at what is now the intersection of the overpass and the interstate, which was removed to make way for the new Interstate 244 (now Interstate 270). Change must occur for a place to remain viable. But hopefully this book, and others like it, will remind readers of the significance, importance, and impact of the people and places that came before us. Without those influences, we would not be who or where we are now.

One

A LONG AND RICH HISTORY

This is the area the locals call Indian Hill. On the southwestern border of the city of Sunset Hills, this area overlooks the Meramec River, seen in the middle, and incorporates Minnie HaHa Beach. Stretching from the riverfront north into the city, the historic Native American period of this site dates back to the 16th or 17th century. Its importance as an Indian site is known worldwide, even back to the prehistoric days. One thing that drew the prehistoric and historic tribes to the area was salt, which was needed to preserve food. Without salt, people would be forced to eat only the food in season in their immediate hunting area. (Courtesy of SHHS.)

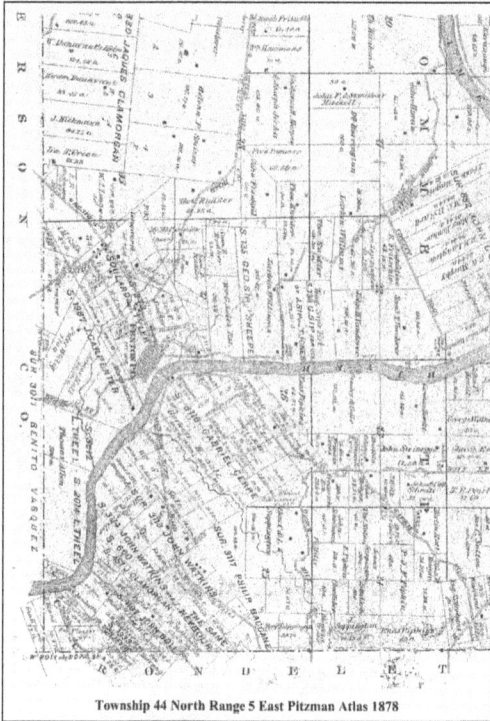

Township 44 North Range 5 East Pitzman Atlas 1878

The 1878 Pitzman Atlas, seen here, detailed landholdings on each side of the Meramec River in the area that includes Sunset Hills. Land is seen under the names Cerre, Clamorgan, and Boli. Purveying salt became both a duty and a profession. Several salt springs were located in the Sunset Hills area. Besides Jacques Clamorgan, who owned a huge salt works, Gabriel Cerre (1733–1805) had a salt spring near what is now West Watson Road on his country property. Cerre was born in Montreal, Canada, and migrated to Illinois by the mid-1750s, where he lived in Kaskaskia for several decades. A merchant, he had acquired quite a large amount of property through Spanish land grants and other means in the St. Louis area by the late 1770s. Cerre moved his wife, Catherine Gerard, and their family to the St. Louis area in 1779 or 1780. Besides his property in what is now Sunset Hills, he owned a house in the city of St. Louis. In 1791, Cerre owned more slaves than anyone else in the area. (Courtesy of SHHS.)

One of Cerre's daughters, Marie Therese Cerre (1769–1842), married Col. Auguste Chouteau (about 1750–1829, pictured at right), who was 20 years her senior. Their marriage united two strong St. Louis mercantile families. Colonel Chouteau was also one of the founders of St. Louis. (Courtesy of SHHS.)

10

Fransisco Luis Hector, Baron de Carondelet (1748–1807) was governor of the Spanish territories of Louisiana and Florida from 1791 to 1797. This area along the Mississippi was known as the Upper Louisiana Territory and was at that time the property of Spain. The Baron de Carondelet (pictured) was succeeded as governor by Manuel Gayoso de Lemos (1747–1799), who served from 1797 until his death in 1799. (Courtesy of SHHS.)

The United States and Spain often disputed borders, especially along the Mississippi. In 1794, Spain closed New Orleans to all products coming down the Mississippi. For the burgeoning town of St. Louis and its merchants, this would have meant disaster in the long term. "Pinckney's Treaty" was ratified by both parties in 1796, establishing US and Spanish colonial borders and promoting friendship between the two countries. Pictured is Thomas Pinckney (1750–1828), a Revolutionary War patriot who was serving as ambassador to the United Kingdom and a special envoy to Spain when he arranged this treaty, also known as the Treaty of San Lorenzo. (Courtesy of SHHS.)

In 1800, Daniel Boone (pictured) arrived in what is now called Missouri and received a tremendous amount of land for himself, his family, and his friends from the Spanish government to become the syndic (judge and jury) and commandant (military leader) of the Femme Osage district—now St. Charles County. Boone's grant was for 1,000 arpents, or 850 acres, plus more for each family he brought with him. The Indian tribal lands south of the Femme Osage district, including the important tribal meeting site of Minnie HaHa, were also under the control of a syndic, who many believe was Jacques Clamorgan, largely because of his tremendous power in the area. (Courtesy of Marc Kollbaum.)

John Sappington (1750–1815), his wife, Jemima Fowler Sappington (1758–1814), and their 17 children made the move with the extended Boone family from Kentucky to the Upper Louisiana Territory. Sappington had served as George Washington's bodyguard at Valley Forge in the Revolutionary War. Most of the Sappington children lived to marry and have children, and many descendants still live in the area. This 1843 lithograph by P. Haas shows General Washington and General Lafayette at Valley Forge in 1777. (Courtesy of LOC: LC-USZ262-819.)

Henry Sheffie Geyer (1790–1859) was born in Maryland and became a lawyer and a US senator. A captain in the War of 1812 in frontier units, Geyer (left) was practicing law in St. Louis by 1815. In 1820, he was a delegate to the Missouri State Constitutional Convention. He also wrote the Geyer Act in 1839, which established public education in Missouri. He declined the post of secretary of war offered to him in 1850 by Pres. Millard Fillmore. Geyer Road in the area is named for him. He was also the attorney for John Sanford, the brother of Irene Sanford Emerson, the widow of Dr. John Emerson, the owner of Dred Scott. Irene Emerson granted ownership of the slave to Sanford after she remarried. Roswell (or Raswell) Martin Field (1807–1869) was the attorney who filed suit in federal court in 1853 on Scott's behalf. Field (right) prepared the case, but another attorney argued it. He is thought to have either lived on or owned property on Weber Hill Road in Sunset Hills. He is also the father of the noted St. Louis poet Eugene Field. (Left, courtesy of the Missouri State Archives; right, courtesy of SHHS.)

Dred Scott (1799–1858) was a slave brought west by the family of Captain Peter Blow (1777–1832) and sold to Dr. John Emerson. Emerson took Scott and the Scott family to non-slave states during his military service. Scott used this time in non-slave states to later argue for his freedom all the way to the Supreme Court, which found against Scott. The children of Peter Blow, with whom Scott had grown up, purchased his freedom from Sanford. Scott died less than a year later. The repercussions of these lengthy trials were felt strongly in the country around St. Louis, including Sunset Hills, where gentleman farmers ran their southern plantations with the help of slaves. (Courtesy of LOC: LC-USZ62-5092.)

DRED SCOTT.

13

Asa Tesson (1823–1902) owned a gristmill and was a gentleman farmer on Denny Road (later renamed Lindbergh Boulevard). He married Ann Stordy (or Sturdy) on December 16, 1849. By 1851, Tesson had built the two-story stone house above on his property. Within two years, Stordy had died, and Tesson married his neighbor, Mathilda Eddie, and they had nine children. Tesson appears on the 1850 Slave Schedule, a part of the census, as owning one nine-year-old male mulatto slave. Other local names on the same page of the schedule included several Wells, Long, and Sappington families. The 1880 funeral of Tesson's 30-year-old daughter Matilda "Mattie" Tesson Clement, wife of Charles, was led from this house. At left is Asa Tesson's 1902 death certificate. (Above, courtesy of SHHS; left, author's collection.)

Col. Frederick Dent (1786–1873) was a neighbor of Asa Tesson's who owned many slaves on his plantation, White Haven, on Gravois Road toward St. Louis. Ulysses S. Grant and Dent's daughter, Julia, were married in 1848 at White Haven. Grant's family, who were abolitionists, did not approve of Dent's ownership of slaves, and boycotted the wedding. Colonel Dent died in the White House in 1873, during his son-in-law's presidency. (Courtesy of Marc Kollbaum.)

Julia Boggs Dent (1826–1902) was away at a boarding school in St. Louis when Ulysses S. Grant first visited White Haven. He had been her brother Frederick Jr.'s roommate at West Point. After their first meeting, Grant often made the trek from Jefferson Barracks to White Haven on horseback. Their engagement was lengthy because of the Mexican War, but they were eventually married in 1848. (Courtesy of LOC: LC-USZ62-101867.)

15

Ulysses S. Grant (1822–1885), the 18th president, made this area his adopted home. Stationed at Jefferson Barracks as a young second lieutenant after West Point, he forged lifelong relationships with many families in the area. His properties are just to the east of modern-day Sunset Hills. Some of these parcels of land now comprise the Ulysses S. Grant National Historic Site, and are run by the National Park Service. (Courtesy of LOC: LC-USZ62-110718.)

This 1970s elementary school class took a field trip to the Log Cabin School on West Watson Road. One snowy night in the 1860s, Gen. Ulysses S. Grant, traveling on horseback, stopped at the school for the evening. In the morning, before he continued on his journey, he penned a note to the school, thanking them for their hospitality. The students, who came to see the former school and read the note, are, from left to right, Angie Bessinger, Pat Bessinger (parent and teacher aid), John Dennis O'Dowd, Sonja Kunzelman, Linda Krumm, John Frederick, unidentified, and Peggy Wahlig. (Courtesy of SHHS.)

The oldest sustained business in the Sunset Hills area began operation in 1912 as a supply store and repair shop, repairing wagon wheels and then cars, before becoming a licensed Ford dealer in 1915. The company, now known as Sunset Auto, is the oldest sustained Ford dealer in Missouri. It was started by Peter Heutel (1871–1927) and the fifth generation of the Heutel family now runs the company. (Courtesy of SHHS.)

As residents experienced the changes that came with the 20th century, Sunset Hills, like many communities around the country, became somewhat more urban than rural. Companies like Rott's General Store, on the corner of Gravois and Sappington Roads; Hunkler Feed Store, on Gravois; and the Eime General Store on Tesson Ferry Road now supplied residents with provisions. But even with the modern conveniences and changes, there were still people interested in preserving the past. In the 1930s, this man with a covered wagon came down West Watson Road to the Log Cabin School, which was by then a private residence, tracing the route the stagecoach took through the area. (Courtesy of SHHS.)

Looking northwest across Route 30 interchange

As we became a more mobile society, additional roads, highways, and interstates were created to accommodate the ever-increasing traffic. The 1960s saw the advent of Interstate 244, now known as Interstate 270, which traveled north and south throughout the western suburbs, including Sunset Hills. Pictured here is the original interchange of I-270 and Gravois Road, now known as Highway 30. (Courtesy of SHHS.)

Overpass at Interstate 44

Pictured here is the interchange on the northwesternmost side of Sunset Hills, at Historic Highway Route 66, as it merges through this parcel as Interstate 44, meeting Interstate 270. (Courtesy of SHHS.)

Two

EARLY FAMILIES

Many of the early families came to the area in the 1840s as immigrants of German, Prussian, or Austro-Hungarian descent. They had surnames like Frederick, Fuchs, Hunkler, Kimker, Koehler, Richardt, Rothweiler, Sieveking, Vogelgesang, Vogt, and Von Eime. The land reminded them of the homes they had left behind. This is a large reunion of the Von Eime family. Some branches of the family have, over the years, eliminated the "Von" from their names, making it just Eime. (Courtesy of SHHS.)

William Von Eime (1838–1909) and his wife, Katherine (about 1840–1916), are the founders of the area's large Von Eime, or Eime, clan. They were early farmers. Their sons were Gottlieb, Henry, August, William, and Charles F. Their daughters were Emily, who married Herman Troegeler; Louise, who married George Schwerz, or Schwarz; and Christina, or "Dina," who married Otto Ude. (Courtesy of SHHS.)

August Eime (1862–1945) and Elizabeth Raaf (1865–1937) are seen here in their formal wedding portrait. (Courtesy of Jill Arnone.)

August and Elizabeth Eime's family grew rapidly, as these two formal portraits illustrate. It appears that the parents, in lieu of posing for an additional formal portrait, elected to paste in a photograph of their eighth child, Edna, at far left below. (Courtesy of SHHS.)

The Eime family had a hardware store and a grocery store in the area. (Courtesy of SHHS.)

This photograph from an early Eime family reunion has the men on a diagonal behind their wives. They are, from left to right, Henry Eime and Josephine Eberhardt Eime; Charles F. Eime and Margaret Schlietz Eime; Otto Ude and Christina "Dina" Eime Ude; Herman Troegler, also known as Teglar and Emily Eime Troegler; George E. Schwerz and Louise Eime Schwerz; August Eime and Elizabeth Raaf Eime; William Eime and Ann Wittemann Eime; and Gottlieb K. Eime and Hulda Bendel Eime. Christine Eime Ude, in the front row, third from the left, was one of the first female pharmacists in the St. Louis area. (Courtesy of SHHS.)

Another family with a long history in the Sunset Hills area is the Frederick family. Their house, located on West Watson Road, was purchased by John E.J. Fredericks from Jemima Head in 1857 for $1,000. A portion of the house's foundation was recently uncovered and showed the date of 1833, making it likely the oldest house in Sunset Hills. John was an immigrant from Hanover, Germany, and six generations of the family have lived on the farm. Pictured below is one of the Frederick descendants and his family. (Above, courtesy of SHHS; below, author's collection.)

The family of George Hunkler (1821–1892), who came from Germany in the mid-1840s, lived on Gravois Road. Six successive generations of the family lived on Hunkler Hill. Seen above is the Hunkler family store. According to the family story, George Hunkler and his two brothers, too poor to purchase passage to America, successfully stowed away on a ship to gain better lives. The Hunkler Feed Store was owned and operated by George's son, George A. (1861–1938), and his wife, Wilhelmine Henrietta Rothweiler (1862–1952). The store, in front of their house, also sold other items, including milk, soda, penny candies, and bait. The building in which the grain and feed were kept is seen below. At one time, there were gasoline pumps in front of the store. (Above, author's collection; below, courtesy of SHHS.)

Louise Sophia "LuLu" Hunkler (1890–1982), daughter of George and Wilhelmine Hunkler, and her husband, Earl Smith (1888–1972), seen at right, are the author's grandparents. Below are Louise's cousin, William Richard (left), and her brother, George F. Hunkler (1891–1952), in their World War I uniforms. After the war, George F. married Mathilda Wagner (1896–1995), whose family owned a large farm across the Meramec River in Fenton. George and Mathilda also settled on Hunkler Hill. (Right, author's collection; below, courtesy of Della Lang.)

This family reunion at Hunkler Hill featured the third, fourth, and fifth generations of the Hunkler family, including, from left to right (first row) Marcella Smith Spitz, Pam Spitz, and Audrey Smith Kitchell; (second row) Louise Hunkler Smith, the author, Hardy Smith, Blanche Smith Baldwin, William Everett Kitchell, Sharon Smith, Mark Albrecht, Bunny Smith, and Jim Spitz; (third row) Betty Jean Smith Albrecht, Milton Spitz, Mike Baldwin, Sherwood Kitchell, and Earl Smith Jr. (Courtesy of Joseph J. Grassino.)

Henry Eime, the son of William and Katherine Von Eime, dropped the "Von" from his surname. This is the Henry Eime and family's splendid three-story Victorian house on Gravois Road adjacent to the Hunkler property. Both properties are now the site of Friendship Village. Henry Eime's farm was considered in its time to be the "model farm" for Missouri. (Courtesy of SHHS.)

Another prominent Sunset Hills family, Frederick W. Eggeling and his wife, Ida Louise Leisse Eggeling, sent all three of their boys—Fred W. Jr. (1893–1958), Hubert Joseph (1895–1947), and Edward Gus (1897–1973)—off to World War I. Pictured here is Hubert, the family's middle son. Before he was drafted in June 1917, Hubert was a sophomore at the University of Missouri, Columbia, majoring in agriculture. He died on May 15, 1947, and is buried in Bellefontaine Cemetery in north St. Louis County. (Both, courtesy of SHHS.)

One of the numerous Richard/Richardt families in the area was the family of George Richard, which included, from left to right, George, Elizabeth, Ben, Lydia, Bill, and Louise Richard. They are one of the original German farming families in the area. (Courtesy of Della Lang.)

This unusual photograph features Louisa Vogelgesang, the daughter of Charles and Louise Vogelgesang, posing in several different ways. Louisa (about 1890–1970) married George Fuchs (about 1886–1980) on April 20, 1920, at Saint Peter Catholic Church in Kirkwood. After the service, they all returned to the Vogelgesang farm. (Courtesy of SHHS.)

Charles (about 1847–1918) and Louise (about
1857–1932) Vogelgesang are seen here. Louise's
last name was probably Dierhault or Deerholt.
Charles was the son of Melchoir Vogelgesang
(1821–1894) and Elizabeth Hilda Heinemann (1817–
1892). The entire family emigrated from Germany
when Charles was a child, arriving in America on
August 27, 1852, on the ship *George Green*. (Courtesy
of SHHS.)

This photograph was taken at a 1961 family reunion of the George Fuchs family. Weddings and family reunions were once considered the social events of the season early in Sunset Hills history. The ever-changing dynamics of the mid 20th century made these large reunions increasingly rare. (Courtesy of SHHS.)

Three

EARLY SCHOOLS, CHURCHES, AND CEMETERIES

Log Cabin School, Rott Road

In 1865, the Log Cabin School opened on what is now West Watson Road, and students filled the schoolhouse until 1884. It was the site of Grant's snowbound visit in 1866. In the late 1800s, the majority of people in the St. Louis area received, at best, a grade-school education. Schools were local, often built by families in small areas where the population was rapidly increasing and a school was needed. Students wishing to continue past eighth grade needed to find transportation to a high school. Those students would attend Kirkwood High School, which opened in 1896, the first four-year high school in St. Louis County. (Courtesy of SHHS.)

Rott School started as a one-room frame schoolhouse near the intersection of Rott and West Watson Roads in 1884, serving the area until 1906 with one teacher. Rather than the current method of grade advancement by year and age, the students progressed by showing proficiency in the "reader" for individual levels. The class of 1899, taught by John Berthold, included, from left to right, (first row) Louise DeGrendele, Augusta Koehler, Margaret Heidel, Helen Wahlig, Anna Bost, Anna Koch, Rosa Schleisner, Minnie Helfert, George Wahlig, and Martin Weber; (second row) Kate Wahlig, Minnie Hunkler, Marie Meyer, Emelia Becker, Rosa Becker, Mollie Meyer, Emelia Koch, Henry "Heine" Hunkler, Will DeGrendele, James Meyer, and Karl Weber; (third row) Sophia Helfert, Yetta Frederick, Lucy DeGrendele, LuLu Hunkler, Clara Schleisner, Clara Longheinrich, unidentified, Maggie Bost, Lulu Hoch, Evelyn Koehler, Luetta Meyer, Walter Lonhenrich, Henry Frederick, and Christ Koehler; (fourth row) Fred Koheler, Fred Wahlig, Charles Wahlig, George F. Hunkler, and unidentified. (Courtesy of SHHS.)

In 1906, Rott School moved to a larger building, referred to as the second Rott School, where it remained until 1931. This class, whose teacher is listed as Miss Dressel, is from between 1905 and 1910. (Courtesy of SHHS.)

34

The second Rott School is seen here between 1907 and 1913. During these years, the school was taught by Miss Selma Kruse, the daughter of the pastor of Saint Lucas Church on Denny Road. Miss Kruse walked from the parsonage on Denny Road to the school on West Watson Road every day. (Courtesy of SHHS.)

This impressive new brick structure, the third Rott School, was dedicated in November 1931. It was a marvel of the time, with multiple rooms and offices upstairs and a kitchen, auditorium, boiler room, and indoor restrooms on the lower floor. There was still no transportation to the school until the late 1930s. (Courtesy of SHHS.)

The class of 1931 posed on the steps of the new school building right after it opened in November 1931. Because of the post–World War II baby boom, Rott School was expanded in 1948, adding additional classrooms and a gymnasium. The boom also changed the way students were educated. After its closure as a public school in 1976, Rott School was used for years as the Judavine Center for Autism. (Courtesy of SHHS.)

The 1919 class of the Concord School included, from left to right, (first row) unidentified, August Juengel, John Krupa, unidentified, L. Niemeier, Clarence Eime, William Ruder, and Alois Wohlschlager; (second row) Edna Eime, Esta Heutel, Amelia Wohlschlager, Mabel Aff, Evelyn Crecelius, Emily Weimer, Martha Wohlschlager, Sadie Juengel, and Auguste Hampe; (third row) Hilda Walker, Lillian ?, teacher Miss Gibson, unidentified, Rowland Wohlschlager, Casper Krupe, Erme Ruder, Laura Juengel, and Cordelia Schuetz. (Courtesy of SHHS.)

Ora Goode Hearon, a Fenton resident who taught for more than four decades at Fenton School (where children from the southwest section of Sunset Hills attended school), was one of the most well-known and best-loved educators in the area. Here, she celebrates her 25th wedding anniversary with her husband, Ernest Hearon. (Courtesy of Bob and Wanda Winter.)

Fenton School, seen here in 1983, had been in the same location on Gravois Road since 1873, on land purchased from the Rudder family. Students from both sides of the Meramec River—Sunset Hills and Fenton—attended this school until its closure in the 1980s. The building was expanded in the 1960s because of a brisk increase in enrollment in the school, largely due to the arrival of the Chrysler plant to Fenton. (Courtesy of Beth Cross and Lindbergh School District.)

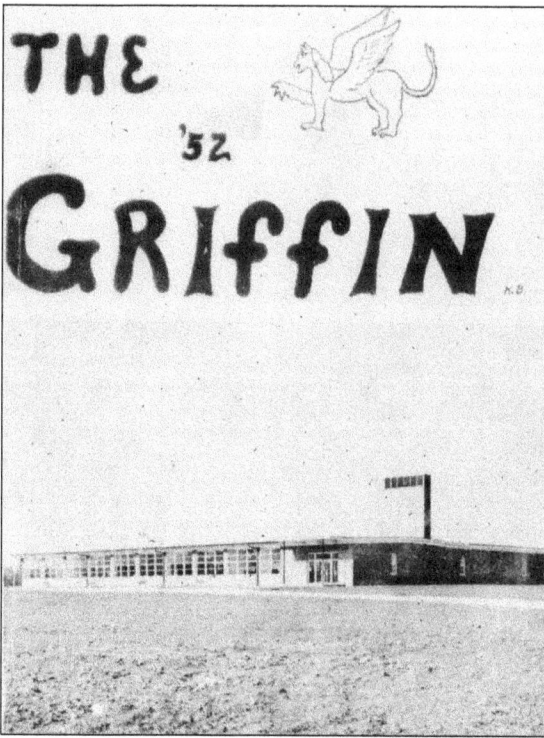

In 1949, Missouri ordered a reorganization of school districts and Concord, Fenton, Grant, Rott, and Sappington Schools joined the newly formed R-8 school district, originally known as Grandview. There was no high school building that first year, 1950–1951, so students met in the basement and boiler room of an elementary school. The mascot, as well as the first yearbook, was the Griffin. The name Grandview met with disapproval, so the high school was renamed Lindbergh in spring 1952 and dedicated on September 14. The school colors of maroon and gold changed to green and gold, and the mascot became the Flyers in honor of the school's namesake, Charles A. Lindbergh. The yearbook and the newspaper, the *Spirit* and the *Pilot*, also reflected the aviator's influence. The high school witnessed its largest period of growth in the 1970s, when each high school class hovered near the 1,000-student mark. (Courtesy of Beth Cross and Lindbergh School District.)

Long Elementary, seen here with its new, updated facade, was named after John Fenton Long and added to the Lindbergh district in 1960. (Author's collection.)

In the late 1960s, Lindbergh constructed its first middle school near the corner of Lindbergh Boulevard and Eddie and Park Road. Known first only as the middle school, it was later named Truman Middle School in honor of the Missouri-born president. Because of the waning enrollment as the baby boomer generation eased, the building became an elementary school and an early childhood education center before recently returning to its original purpose as a middle school. (Courtesy of SHHS.)

The 1970–1971 school year saw the advent of the Robert H. Sperreng Middle School on Tesson Ferry Road. Its namesake served as president of the board for 13 of his 15 years on the Lindbergh School District Board of Education, from 1955 to 1970. (Courtesy of Beth Cross and Lindbergh School District.)

ROBERT H. SPERRENG MIDDLE SCHOOL
12111 Tesson Ferry Road, St. Louis, Missouri
LINDBERGH SCHOOL DISTRICT

On Lindbergh Boulevard, nestled behind a brush of trees, stands the Thomas Jefferson School. It is a small school accepting both boarding and day students in grades 7–12. Charles E. Merrill, the son of one of the Merrill Lynch cofounders, was one of the school's founders in 1946. Originally designed as a boys 9–12 prep school with high academic standards, the school became coeducational in 1971. An eighth grade program was added in 1976, and a seventh grade followed in 1981. Robin McCoy, another of the school's founders, was the school's headmaster for 34 years. Pictured is the front of the school facing Lindbergh Boulevard. (Courtesy of SHHS.)

Washington School chose to join the Mehlville school district during the 1949 reformation of districts. In this 1930s photograph, Sunset Hills–area children perform the school play *Tom Thumb's Wedding.* (Courtesy of SHHS.)

Early settlers had to travel long distances to attend church. French and Spanish Catholics were among the earliest settlers to the area and had to travel to Saint Peter Catholic Church in Kirkwood, whose first two churches were built about 1843 and 1867, or to Fenton to attend Saint Paul, which was established in 1878. The Concord Baptist Church began services around 1809, but by the end of the 1840s, much of the Sunset Hills area was populated by Germans, who attended Saint John Evangelist Kirsch and parsonage, constructed in 1838. It was the first Evangelist church of the North American Synod, as a monument in the churchyard announces. (Courtesy of SHHS.)

Notice that this Bender tombstone, in the St. John cemetery, uses the words for Mother and Father in the family's native German tongue. A Bender relative's monument nearby carries the same endearments in English. This captures the feeling of the area: many immigrants chose to maintain their native heritage and language, while many—often in the same family—decided to embrace their new country and its language. (Courtesy of Shelly Minnella.)

Within four decades, the sizable congregation at Saint John warranted the establishment of a second evangelical church. Interested parties met on March 1, 1880, and a constitution and bylaws were accepted on March 29, 1880. Saint Lucas Church was built on Denny Road and dedicated on July 24, 1881. This first church was a frame building on five acres, which was replaced with this stone building in 1905, with stone quarried on Gravois Road. A Mr. Bopp was the general contractor and the dedication coincided with the 25th anniversary of the original dedication. The campus, including the cemetery, is now over 30 acres and the church is now Saint Lucas United Church of Christ. (Courtesy of SHHS.)

One of the yearly activities for area children in the 1950s and 1960s was attending Vacation Bible School at St. Lucas. This 1957 class included children aged three and four. (Author's collection.)

This Vacation Bible School class from June 1957 features the author in the first row, second from right, and her cousin, Keven G. Wilke, in the second row, second from left. (Author's collection.)

In 1973, the Saint Lucas Cemetery incorporated the adjacent Park Hill Cemetery and the old name was discontinued. The joint cemetery now has over 2,500 interments with a variety of monuments and grave markers. Among the most unusual is the tall tree-shaped monument to James L. Kennerly (1810–1871) and Francis L. Kennerly (1822–1874) at left. The obelisk at right is one of the tallest in the cemetery, erected in memory of Fred C. Schwentker (1850–1901). (Author's collection.)

This arch-shaped monument, with each leg bearing information, commemorates Mathias Rothweiler (1830–1912) and Katherina Sinde Rothweiler (1838–1922). (Author's collection.)

Saint Thomas/Holy Spirit Lutheran Church on Lindbergh Boulevard was founded in 1962 and is a member of the Evangelical Lutheran Church of America. (Courtesy of SHHS.)

Saint Justin Martyr Catholic Church was created in 1964 as a new parish in the Sunset Hills area on Eddie and Park Road. Work began on the new church in 1965, and the first school year in the parish began in the fall of 1966. Father Joseph Albrecht was the church's first priest. (Courtesy of SHHS.)

Outside the city limits of Sunset Hills in the neighboring municipality of Crestwood is the Sappington Cemetery. It was originally known as the Long Cemetery, being the resting place of Judge John Long, the son-in-law of John S. Sappington and his wife, Jemima Fowler Sappington. The Sappingtons had 17 children, nine of whom are also buried here. The Sappington patriarch was a sergeant in the Revolutionary War, and was with George Washington at Valley Forge. John's grave has been marked by both the John Sappington Chapter, National Society, Daughters of the American Revolution (DAR) and by a society of Valley Forge descendants. (Courtesy of Leslie Vander Meulen Canavan.)

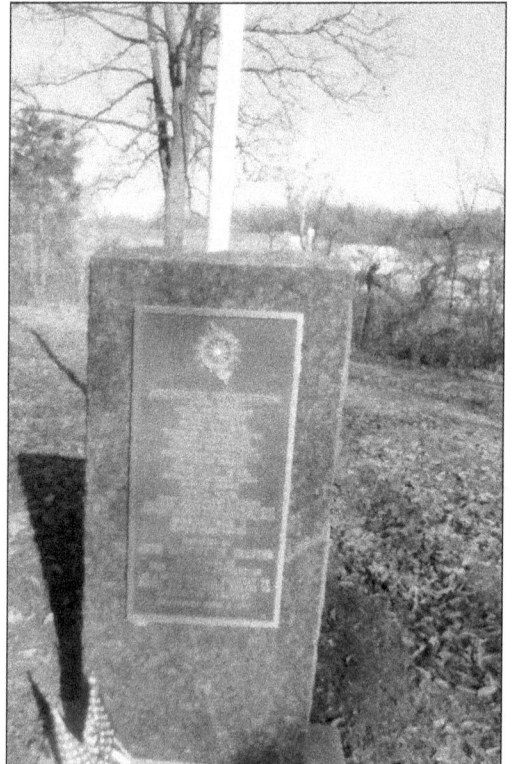

Also in the Sappington Cemetery is a "Soldiers' Memorial," erected in 1975 after the DAR restored the cemetery. The cemetery features three Revolutionary War heroes—John Sappington, Joseph Wells, and Judge John Long; five veterans from the War of 1812—William Lindsay Long, John Sappington, Thomas Sappington, Zephaniah Sappington, and Richard Wells; two Mexican War veterans—Thomas Sanford Long and Samuel Parke; three Civil War veterans—John Sappington Parke, Thomas Jefferson Sappington, and Henry Fenton Steinhaver, M.D.; and one from World War I—Mauro Eads Smith. The cemetery is owned and maintained by the City of Crestwood. (Author's collection.)

Thomas Eddie (1799–1894) was a Scottish immigrant to the area. A merchant and explorer, Eddie joined fur trappers with the Rocky Mountain Fur Expedition in 1823. He returned in 1827, and, according to the story, traded his "store bought boots" for land. All together, he amassed around 370 acres. In 2008, Jane Hake's fourth grade class at Truman Elementary engaged in a cemetery project to help clean up Eddie Cemetery, just a little outside of Sunset Hills in Sappington. During this process, a new granite sign was erected to mark the site. (Left, courtesy of John Maurath; right, courtesy of Amy Grassino.)

In this view of the small Eddie Cemetery, the burial site of Thomas Eddie and his wife, Margaret Clark Eddie (1814–1892), is the large monument in the rear center. When many of the burials in this cemetery occurred, it was not legal to bury an African American in a white cemetery. The Eddies, who were slaveowners before the Civil War, buried their slaves outside the limits of the cemetery itself, on the other side of the fence lines surrounding the cemetery. (Courtesy of Amy Grassino.)

To honor the slaves buried outside the borders of Eddie Cemetery, Jane Hake's fourth grade class created this space of reflection, calling it the "Secret Garden" and dedicating it to the slaves. (Courtesy of Amy Grassino.)

This broken tombstone adorns the grave of Margaret Eddie (1801–1837), the wife of James Eddie. Their two children, Thomas, six; and James, one, are also mentioned on the tombstone. (Courtesy of Amy Grassino.)

Four

RAIN, SNOW, AND ICE

Weather has gotten the best of Sunset Hills at times, and floods are common along the southwest section of the city near the Meramec River. Two of the most severe floods happened in this section in the 1940s. In 1943 and 1945, floodwaters reached as far east on Gravois Road as the Sieveking and Hunkler properties. There were also very serious floods in 1990 and 1993. Pictured here is the area around Rock Alva Road, which fronts the Meramec River, during the flood of 2009. (Courtesy of the City of Sunset Hills, Trish Moore.)

The flood of 1993 was one of the most severe in the history of the area. This photograph was taken from the Sunset Lakes golf course. (Courtesy of Wayne Ortmann.)

Minnie HaHa Park in Sunset Hills was opened in 2005 and flooded in the spring of 2008. (Author's collection.)

Hardy and Velda Callaway Smith pose with the snowman the family just made in the late 1950s. Living on a hill, building a large snowman was fairly easy. (Courtesy of Joseph J. Grassino.)

While ice makes travel treacherous, it adds splendor and a sense of fantasy when it adorns trees like this one in Sunset Hills. (Courtesy of SHHS.)

Five

RECREATION

The beach at Minnie HaHa brought tourists, residents, and people from St. Louis to the Sunset Hills area. The area was first a prehistoric Native American site, then an Indian trading post and meeting place, and was now serving as a recreational area. In the late 1800s and early 1900s, people swarmed to Minnie HaHa Beach to escape the tremendous heat of the city and cool down in the Meramec River. Later, after buses replaced the trolleys, dedicated buses spent the weekends transporting residents back and forth from St. Louis to Minnie HaHa Beach. This 1916 photograph shows Ann Fisher Callaway, age 18, sitting on the Meramec River bridge just below the beach, on a trip she and her family made nearly every weekend during the sizzling St. Louis summers. (Author's collection.)

Henry Otto poses in his boat across the river from Minnie HaHa. Behind him are the white birch trees that once lined the shore near the beach. (Courtesy of SHHS.)

The beach at Minnie HaHa had a lot to offer its guests, including a dancehall, seen here during high water. The dancehall, like most of the vacation and resident homes along both sides of the riverbank, was built on stilts. Often, people in the clubhouses would boat down to the beach. The building also contained slot machines for many years. (Courtesy of SHHS.)

Minnie HaHa Beach owner Henry Otto stands in front of the large refreshment hall at the beach. (Courtesy of SHHS.)

Henry's son, Fred Otto, stands in front of the refreshment hall. The Otto family sold the tourist attraction to the Other family, who ran it until the late 1950s. For several years after its closure, groups of gypsies would camp on the beach from time to time. (Courtesy of SHHS.)

The traffic on the beach and in the water was so heavy in the early 1950s that Minnie HaHa Beach got its own branch of the Missouri Water Patrol. The 1952 patrol squad included, from left to right, J. Weber, C. Blitt, J. Bruen, G. Aurin, R. Meeks, W. Hausknecht, B. Kunnhenn,

D. Finazzi, G. Ross, C. Strele, R. Lindsay, G. Bell, R. Mueller, B. Johaller, F. Jostrand, J. Cronin, R. Stuecken, C. Schrimpf, E. Couch, G.W. Hook, A. Bingeheimer, W. Lundt, W. Weseloh, H. Queensen, and K. Stumpf. (Courtesy of SHHS.)

Sunset Inn with Sunset Hill Country Club to the right, Denney and Gravois Roads, St. Louis Co., Mo.

Adolphus Busch (1842–1913), of Anheuser-Busch fame, thought the south county area could use a club for dining and socialization. In November 1910, he opened a club on a 26-acre tract of land and within a few years, Sunset Inn boasted nearly 2,000 members. In 1911, Busch acquired more land and opened the Sunset Hill Country Club. The location noted, at Denney and Gravois Roads, has since changed, when Denney Road became Lindbergh Boulevard. Eventually, Sunset Inn and Sunset Hill Country Club merged, becoming Sunset Country Club. The club celebrated its centennial in 2011. (Both, courtesy of SHHS.)

Interior of Sun Set Inn, St. Louis, Mo.

The text on this postcard describes this as the rustic dining veranda at the Sunset Inn. (Courtesy of SHHS.)

August A. Busch (1865–1934) was the son of Adolphus and Elizabeth "Lilly" Anheuser Busch (1844–1928.) The younger Busch ran the brewing company from after his father's death in 1913 until 1934. He was a great hunter, doing quite a bit of it at the club in Sunset Hills, shooting a total of eight owls, including the one shown here, on the grounds in 1911 or 1912. The owls have been displayed in the club ever since. (Courtesy of Jim Healey and Sunset Country Club.)

This 1926 aerial view of Sunset Country Club provides a clear view of the golf course and the Geyer Road entrance to the club. Lindbergh Boulevard (formerly Denny Road) begins at the top center, winding down past the club. Gravois Road runs horizontally in the lower third of the photograph. Sunset's million-gallon reservoir, at left center, was used to supply water to the club and golf course before the club was connected to the county water supply. The club's saltwater pool is believed to be the first outdoor swimming pool in the area. (Courtesy of Jim Healey and Sunset Country Club.)

With the increase in automobiles in the area, more people—even women, as seen here—began driving. (Courtesy of SHHS.)

Hunkler boys and their friends brought their motorcycles to Hunkler Hill to ride on the fields. (Courtesy of Della Lang.)

Girls in Sunset Hills did not let the boys have all the fun where sports were concerned. In this 1938 photograph, five-year-old Audrey Eime is the batgirl seated in front. (Courtesy of Jill Arnone.)

Bowling has always been a favorite pastime in Sunset Hills. This bowling team from the mid-1960s included, from left to right, (kneeling) Frances Engelman and Alice Wasser; (standing) Marie Tarrant, Marcella Smith Spitz, Velda Callaway Smith, and Sharon Steinhart. (Courtesy of Joseph J. Grassino.)

Along with the great golf links at Sunset Country Club, there are two courses across from each other on West Watson Road, Tapawingo (above) and the former Sunset Lakes, now Sunset Hills Golf Course and Banquet Center (right). Tapawingo contains three nine-hole courses and was designed by Gary Player. According to some, the league pictured at right was the best to have played at Sunset Lakes. (Above, author's collection; right, courtesy of Wayne Ortmann.)

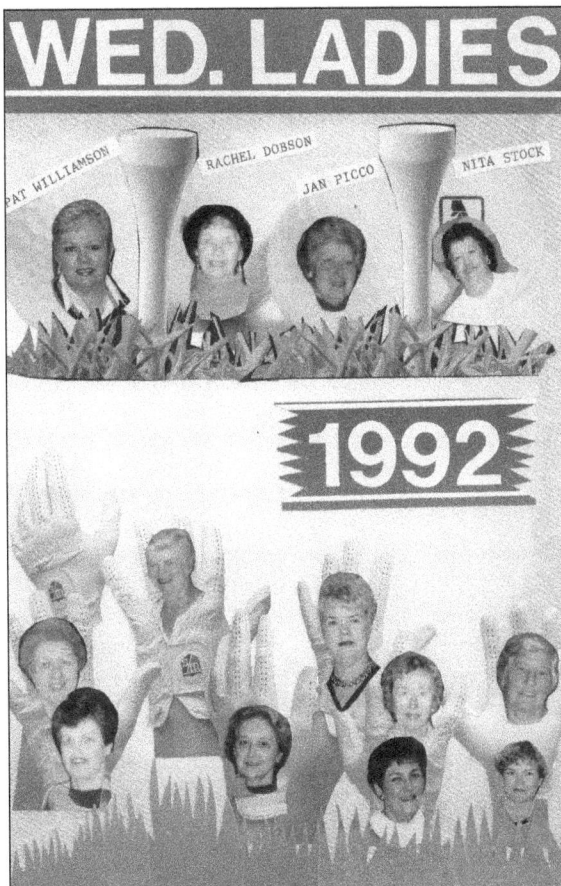

WED. LADIES

PAT WILLIAMSON   RACHEL DOBSON   JAN PICCO   NITA STOCK

1992

63

Real estate broker Henry H. Laumeier married Matilda Cramer in 1941. After purchasing this property from Roland Kahle's widow, Ada, the Laumeiers made the estate their country home. They planted specimen trees and enlarged the property to 72 acres. In 1975, the property was turned into a park. After St. Louis artist Ernest Trevo donated 40 sculptures to the park in 1976, the park, now known as Laumeier Sculpture Park, became extremely popular with both residents and tourists. (Courtesy of Laumeier Sculpture Park Archives.)

Visitors to Laumeier Sculpture Park get a close-up look at Tony Tasset's 12-foot-diameter "Eye" in 2007. (Photograph courtesy of Mike Venso and Laumeier Sculpture Park.)

Laumeier Sculpture Park boasts an internationally recognized collection of sculpture, including Mark di Suvero's "Bornibus," made in 1985–1987, at left. Temporary exhibitions are hosted in the indoor galleries in the Estate House, built by Roland Kahle in 1917. (Courtesy of Mike Venso and Laumeier Sculpture Park.)

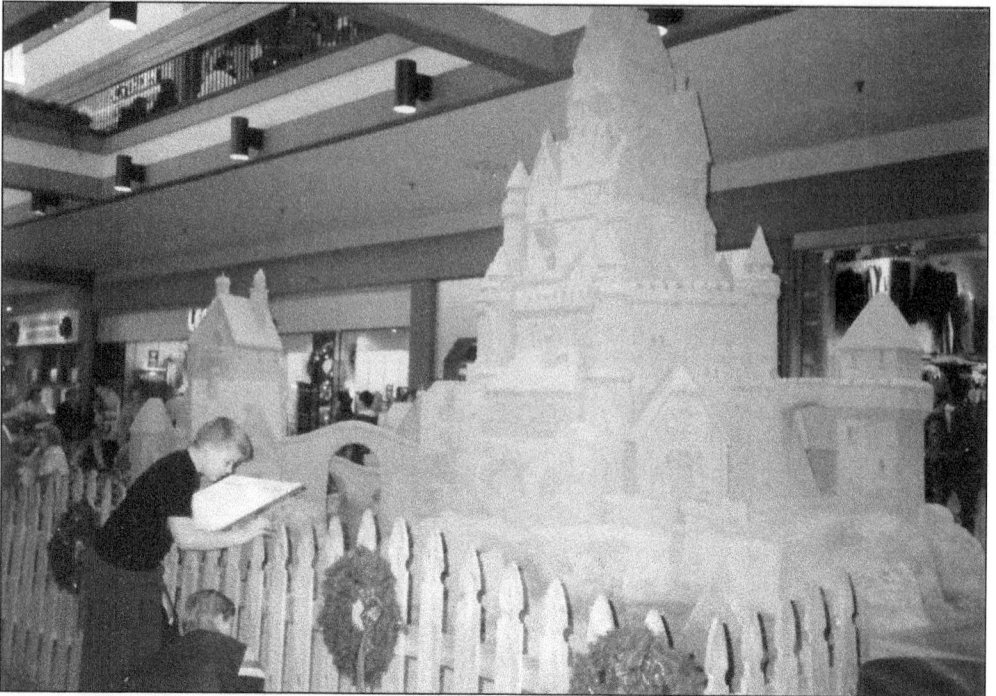

The sand along the Meramec River is considered to be among the best in the country. In 1992, Sand Sculptors International of Redondo Beach, California, spent 300 hours, from November 17 through November 27, constructing this Santa Claus Christmas sand castle at South County Mall. Constructed from 35 tons of Missouri sand from the Winter brothers land, the castle was taken down in the week of January 4, 1993. (Courtesy of Bob and Wanda Winter.)

Baby boomers looked forward to seasonal activities for recreation. In this 1958 photograph, the author is ready to go trick-or-treating with her cousins, Keven G. Wilke (1954–1994) and Randy Wilke. Unfortunately, living on Hunkler Hill, the cousins only had each other's houses at which to trick-or-treat. (Author's collection.)

Children in Sunset Hills and the surrounding area looked forward each October to the annual spook house at Sappington Garden Shop, seen here in 1966. Local schools even took field trips to this annual event. (Courtesy of Sappington Garden Shop.)

The Claire Gempp Davidson Memorial Conservation Area is a nature preserve in the northeast section of the city. The Gempp girls, Marjory and Claire, were related to the Laumeiers. Marjory Elizabeth Gempp (1909–1992) donated the land for the preserve in honor of her late sister, Claire Gempp Davidson. The area is a cooperative effort between the city of Sunset Hills, the Lindbergh School District, and the Missouri Conservation Department. (Author's collection.)

The Claire Gempp Davidson Memorial Conservation Center is not the only park in Sunset Hills; others include Lynstone Park, Minnie HaHa Park, and Watson Trails Park. There are also five athletic fields and an aquatic center in the city. Shown here is the historical marker placed at the conservation center. (Author's collection.)

Six

ALONG THE MAIN THOROUGHFARES

West Watson Road begins at Gravois Road (Highway 30) just above the Meramec River. Originally, West Watson extended all the way to Old Gravois Road, but when the new Highway 30 was built, West Watson's origination was changed to the new highway. One of the things most remembered about this road was the small bridge just around the bend from the intersection at Rock Alva Road. If a vehicle maneuvered the road correctly, gaining a little speed would give passengers the sensation of being airborne. This is an ironic condition as the site facing that bridge—now a golf course—used to be a small landing strip in the 1930s and 1940s. It has not been proven, but locals say that this is one of several area landing strips Charles Lindbergh used on occasion. (Courtesy of Wayne Ortmann.)

The Griesedieck brothers were German immigrants who ran three area breweries. Their beers included Falstaff and Stag. The Griesedieck Carriage House and Stable, on West Watson Road at Rock Alva Road, was later donated by the Griesedieck family to the Paraclete Fathers as a retreat. It later became St. Michael's Retreat for Priests. Sunset Hills resident Alwal Anheuser Moore purchased the property to preserve its natural aspects and prevent it from being subdivided. (Both, courtesy of John Maurath.)

The home of Jacob Rott, for whom Rott Road is named, is one of the most noticeable houses on the street. (Courtesy of SHHS.)

This log cabin school was no longer used as a school when this photograph was taken in the 1920s. (Courtesy of SHHS.)

Another main thoroughfare in Sunset Hills is Kennerly Road, which features houses of every size, from subdivisions to estates. The Kennerly name is a familiar one in the area, going back to Samuel Kennerly of Virginia, a Revolutionary War hero. He moved here in the 1800s to be with his sons, James and George. From 1817 on, they were merchants in the area, and they were appointed as the first sutlers of Jefferson Barracks in 1827. James married Eliza Maria Saugrain in 1817. George Hancock Kennerly, seen here, married Alzire Menard in 1825. Along with being sutler, he was also appointed postmaster of the barracks in 1828. An Army captain, George Hancock Kennerly also had a fondness for duels. (Courtesy of Kedrick Kennerly and the Kennerly Family Archives.)

BRIDGE OVER MERAMEC BUILT IN 192

Gravois Road spans the entire length of Sunset Hills from the Meramec River to Sappington. The road itself is also of historic value. The first written reference to it appears in 1804. The name's meaning, from the French, is disputed, although most believe it is from words meaning "gravelly creek." Prior to being named Gravois, the road was known as "The Road that leads to the Salt Spring of Clamorgan in a Wagon." Because it could accommodate a wagon, it was known as a "big" road. It was the first road in the area to be macadamized—a combination of tar and gravel—in 1845, and in 1914, it became the first concrete-surface road in St. Louis County. Above is a photograph of the 1925 bridge over the Meramec on Gravois Road. Below is a pencil drawing of the same structure by local artist and architect Ed Thias. The bridge was demolished in March 2010 and replaced with an uncovered bridge. (Both, courtesy of SHHS.)

George "Pappy" Winter is seen here with his sons, Bob and Pete. Winter's first wife, Sarah Goode Winter, passed away in 1938, when her children were still teenagers, after which George married his second wife, Viola. George Winter Park in Fenton is named in his honor. Since 1946, George's two sons owned and operated Winter Brothers Material Company on Gravois Road at the Meramec River. Pictured below is a large crane with a scoop unloading sand from a barge. The sand on this part of the Meramec Beach was donated for several summers to Laumeier Sculpture Park to create sand sculptures. (Courtesy of Bob and Wanda Winter.)

Up Gravois Road, past the Highway 30/ Interstate 270 intersection, is Hadley Hill Road, where the former home of the Mill Hill Fathers was located. Adolphus Busch originally had it built for his wife, Florence Parker Lambert, of the Lambert family for which Lambert Airport was named. Busch named the estate Grandview. Mrs. Busch had two sons who were avid airplane pilots and good friends of Charles Lindbergh who helped him prepare for his historic 1927 flight across the Atlantic. There was also a landing strip on their estate, and Lindbergh visited often, using the strip to land. Mrs. Busch willed the property to the Mill Hill Fathers. The estate, which included the main house, stables, and a grotto, was demolished in the early 1990s and replaced by a subdivision of luxury houses. Above, directly across the street from the Mill Hill Fathers, was the sprawling estate of Willis Hadley, owner of Hadley Dean Glass Company, and Jacqueline Busch Jones. The estate also includes August Busch's historic hunting and riding club. Hadley was one of the first aldermen in the city of Sunset Hills. The Hadleys had three children who grew up on the property. At right is the hunting and fishing lodge on the estate. (Both, courtesy of SHHS.)

Sunset Hills Auto Repair Company was started in 1912 by Peter S. Heutel. Early on, Gravois Road in front of the store was still macadamized. The company repaired wagon wheels as well as automobiles. By the time this photograph was taken in 1929, Gravois Road, paved with concrete by then, was a main thoroughfare for automobiles. Eventually, the two-lane road increased to four. (Courtesy of SHHS.)

The auto service department of the original building is seen here. (Courtesy of SHHS.)

This complex at the corner of Gravois and Sappington Barracks Roads included a gas station and Sunset Auto, which has been run by five generations of the Heutel family since its inception in 1912. Although it has moved to the other end of the block from this original location, it still remains—into its second century—an iconic family-owned Sunset Hills company. (Both, SHHS.)

One day in 1944, Johnny Loeffelman, a young meat cutter from St. Louis, was going fishing and stopped at Rott's General Store at Gravois and Sappington Road. But instead of just buying fishing supplies, he bought the store, renaming it Johnny's Market. Although Sunset Hills officially ends across the street from the store, Johnny's Market has been, since its inception, the supermarket of choice and the source of many memories for numerous Sunset Hills residents. In the late 1950s and early 1960s, the store sold records—both 45s and albums—in the front of the store. (Courtesy of Debbie Loeffelman and Johnny's Market.)

Johnny's Market has changed in appearance several times over the years and through remodeling and expansion, it now totals 20,000 square feet. (Courtesy of Debbie Loeffelman and Johnny's Market.)

Several miles east on Gravois Road toward St. Louis is the 870-acre Busch estate. Fronting the road is the hand-built former residence of Ulysses S. and Julia Dent Grant and their family. The Grants referred to this two-story structure as Hardscrabble. It consisted of two rooms on each floor. It was originally built in a different location, which is now part of St. Paul Churchyard Cemetery and was marked with a historic marker by the Webster Groves Chapter, NSDAR. Julia Dent Grant was not happy in the house. Following her mother's death in 1857, the Grant family moved back to the White Haven estate with Colonel Dent. The Grants never lived in Hardscrabble again. It went through several owners in the next decades and was sold to the C.F. Blanke Coffee Company in 1903, dismantled, and reassembled at the St. Louis World's Fair— the Louisiana Purchase Exposition. Following the fair, its fate was in jeopardy and it was expected to be torn down on the site, but in 1907, August A. Busch purchased the two-story house and moved it to his massive estate. Over 200 acres of the Busch estate had been part of the Dent/Grant estate. Above is a close-up of Hardscrabble. Visible in the front yard is a Civil War cannon. Below is the fencing in front of Hardscrabble at Grant's farm. The posts of the fence were constructed from barrels of Civil War rifles. (Both courtesy of SHHS.)

In 1927, the *Watchman Advocate*, a local newspaper, held a contest for the best way to honor Charles A. Lindbergh following his successful solo flight across the Atlantic Ocean. The winner of the contest was John J. Rott, who suggested that the aviator be honored by a highway named after him encircling the city of St. Louis. That became Lindbergh Boulevard, and it is, because of its original purpose, the longest road in St. Louis. (Courtesy of LOC: LC-B2-5897-15.)

The Asa Tesson farm and homestead were replaced with the Fox Meadows subdivision on Lindbergh Boulevard just north of Denny Road. These stone markers adorn the entrance. (Courtesy of SHHS.)

A man owned land on Lindbergh Boulevard and his neighbor across the street paid someone not to take his land to widen the road. The original man, who lost a great bit of his land, erected this Fina gas station fronting the road, directly across from his neighbor's beautiful home. (Courtesy of SHHS.)

The House of Maret, a German-style restaurant on Lindbergh Boulevard for many decades, was on the Maret property just down the street from the family house. Wilhelm August Maret (about 1840–1914) emigrated from Germany in 1870. He married a young widow and they had five children, only one of whom, Charles, lived past the age of three. Charles married Anna Vogelgesang and after the stock market crash of 1929, he let one of his sons, William, take over a small gas station fronting Lindbergh Boulevard. In the next few years, the station added automotive repair and a small store. After Prohibition was repealed in the 1930s, the store started selling beer. Fresh sandwiches were served in the early 1950s, and the House of Maret was born. It became a well-respected restaurant in the area, known for its German cuisine. The space is now occupied by Growler's Pub, which has maintained the House of Maret's striking Tudor façade and its renowned beer garden. (Courtesy of SHHS.)

The Viking Hotel, at the corner of Watson Road (Historic Route 66) and Lindbergh Boulevard, has been the site of countless wedding receptions, conferences, meetings, and other events for decades. Now the Holiday Inn St. Louis-Southwest, most locals still refer to it as the Viking. (Courtesy of SHHS.)

Here are two views of the overpass at Lindbergh Boulevard and Watson Road (Historic Highway 66), the first of its kind in the St. Louis area. It was also among the first of its kind in Missouri, and became the model for interchanges for years to come. (Courtesy of SHHS.)

Steak'N'Shake is near the northern edge of the city on Lindbergh Boulevard, next to the Viking. Two of the restaurant's early carhops are pictured in the c. 1951–1952 photograph below. (Courtesy of Ann Portell Schmitz.)

Seven

SUNSET HILLS RESIDENTS OF NOTE

Adolphus Busch (1842–1913) was the second of 22 children born to Ulrich and Barbara Busch in Germany. Adolphus and three of his brothers immigrated to America in 1857 and he married Lily Anheuser, daughter of Eberhard Anheuser, owner of the Anheuser and Company brewery in St. Louis. Upon Anheuser's death in 1880, Busch changed the name to the Anheuser Busch Company. He enjoyed time in what he called the country, which is now Sunset Hills, building both the Sunset Inn and Sunset Country Club as well as a country estate there. (Courtesy of SHHS.)

William Lemp Jr. (1867–1922) became president of the Lemp Brewery in St. Louis after his father's death, but Prohibition took its toll on the business and it was sold in 1922. Not long after, Lemp (left) committed suicide in his office. His first wife, Lillian Handlan Lemp (below, 1877–1960), was known as the Lavender Lady for her fondness for everything that color, including clothing. The two had a horrible divorce and custody battle in 1909. The judge gave full custody of their only son, William III, to his mother Lillian. His father only received visitations. (Left, courtesy of St. Louis Public Library; below, courtesy of SHHS.)

In 1915, Lemp married Ellie Limberg, the widowed daughter of fellow St. Louis brewer Caspar Koehler of Columbia Brewing Company. Lemp built the expansive Swiss-style chalet below off of Mentz Hill Road. Designed by the staff architect of the brewery, it was estimated to cost around $300,000. (Both, courtesy of SHHS.)

Edward J. Thias (left, with his wife, Doris Thias) was an architect, author, accomplished artist of watercolors and drawings, and a teacher. He designed 650 projects in five states. Doris researched and edited many of his written pieces, including articles, calendars, and books. An artist who excelled in pencil drawings, it is appropriate that his portrait here be one of his pencil drawings. Below is the front cover of the Sunset Hills 50th Anniversary Celebration calendar in 2007, which featured a compilation of his pencil drawings. (Courtesy of SHHS.)

SUNSET HILLS 2007
50TH ANNIVERSARY CELEBRATION

A COMMEMORATIVE CALENDAR OF THE SUNSET HILLS HISTORICAL SOCIETY
Drawings by Edward J. Thias

290 Year Old White Oak Tree on Roosevelt Drive in Sunset Hills, Missouri

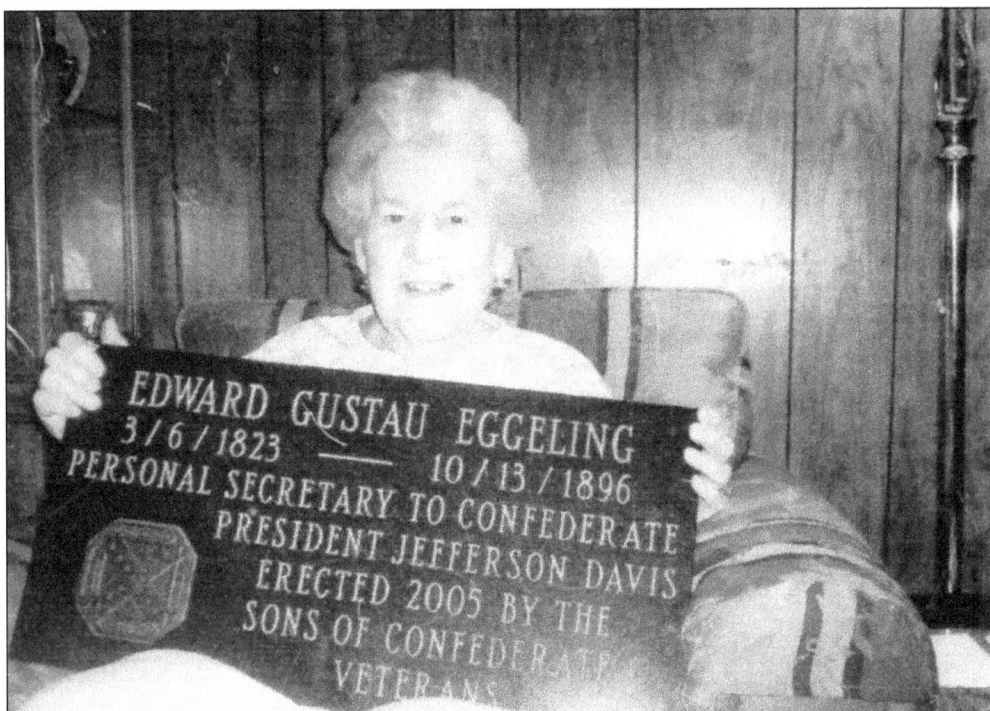

Edward Gustau Eggeling never formally lived in Sunset Hills, but his descendants did. There is even a road in Sunset Hills, Eggeling Lane, named in his honor. During the Civil War, Eggeling was the personal assistant of Jefferson Davis, the president of the Confederate States of America. As the family story goes, Davis presented Eggeling with his own personal walking stick as a thank you for his service. Eggeling's great-granddaughter, Marge Schwaninger, holds a plaque honoring her famous ancestor. (Courtesy of John Maurath.)

Jefferson Davis (1808–1889) also spent time in the St. Louis area: He was one of the officers who escorted Chief Black Hawk to Jefferson Barracks following the Black Hawk War in the 1830s. (Courtesy of Carondelet Historical Society.)

Edward Eggeling's son, Frederick (1864–?), poses with his bride, Ida Louise Leisse (1869–1964). They are the progenitors of the Eggeling clan in the area and had four children: Fred Jr., Hubert Joseph, Edward Gus, and Florence. (Courtesy of John Maurath.)

William Lindsay Long (1789–1849), an early area settler, was an ensign in the War of 1812. He married Elizabeth Sappington (1789–1849), one of the 17 children of John and Jemima Fowler Sappington, in 1808. The Long family built White Haven farm, later owned by Ulysses S. Grant. In 1818, Long bought over 400 acres across the Meramec River from Sunset Hills, intending to sell off 80 small parcels in an eight-square-block area to create a new town. He named the town Fenton after his Welsh grandmother, Elizabeth Fenton Bennett, and moved his family there, selling White Haven to Col. Frederick Dent. By the end of 1820, after selling very few lots in Fenton, Long and his family moved back across the river to Pardee Road, near their old home. In 1849, Long contracted cholera after visiting a sick friend in St. Louis and he, his wife, a daughter, and a daughter-in-law all contracted the disease and died. (Courtesy of SHHS.)

One of William and Elizabeth Long's children was John Fenton Long (1816–1888), who married three times: first to Francis "Fannie" Pipkin (1820–1863) in 1836; then to Pamela Lanham in 1864; and to Mary Nelson Sappington in 1869. Long, known as "Fent," was a schoolteacher, teaching Julia Dent among others. From 1841 to 1842, he was a deputy marshal under Capt. George Kennerly. Long served as Grant's representative in St. Louis while Grant was president. In 1874, Grant appointed Long a surveyor and collector of customs and disbursing agent for the Port of St. Louis. Long Elementary School, opened in 1960, is named in his honor. (Courtesy of Long Elementary School, Lindbergh School District.)

Joseph Michael Medwick (1911–1975) was a baseball player who began and ended his major league career with the St. Louis Cardinals. Born in New Jersey, he played with the Cardinals from 1932 until 1940, becoming a member of the Cardinals during the famous "Gas House Gang" era. Medwick was named to the All-Star team 10 times and was on the 1934 World Series–winning team. In 1937, he was named the National League's Most Valuable Player and scored a National League triple crown. After several years with other teams, Medwick returned to the Cardinals, finishing out his career there in the 1948 season. Throughout his career, he endured the nickname "Ducky" or "Ducky Wucky," which he did not particularly like. Medwick preferred the nickname "Muscles." He was inducted into the Baseball Hall of Fame in 1968. (Courtesy of SHHS.)

Joseph Medwick married Isabelle Heutel (1917–2005) on August 24, 1936, in St. Louis. Her father, Joseph Heutel, gave the couple this house on Geyer Road. "Ducky" Medwick died of a heart attack in St. Petersburg, Florida, on March 21, 1975, at the age of 63. His body was returned to the St. Louis area for burial in Saint Lucas Cemetery in Sunset Hills. (Courtesy of SHHS.)

Bernard Francis "Barney" Dickmann (1888–1971) was the 34th mayor of St. Louis, from 1933 to 1941. Coming to office during the Depression, Dickmann accomplished quite a bit during his two terms as mayor, including the acquisition of land along the riverfront that would eventually become the home of the Gateway Arch and the Jefferson National Expansion Memorial. After his terms as mayor ended, he was appointed the postmaster of St. Louis, a position he held from 1943 to 1958. After his time as mayor, Dickmann lived at least part time in his country home on Hunkler Hill until the late 1950s or early 1960s. He is seen above with his friend, Pres. Harry S. Truman, at Union Station in St. Louis as Truman displays the famous "Dewey Defeats Truman" newspaper. The Poplar Street Bridge, spanning the Mississippi River in St. Louis, is officially named the Bernard F. Dickmann Memorial Bridge. (Courtesy of Harry S. Truman Presidential Library.)

Lyle J. Bouck, born in 1923, was a child of the Depression in the Sunset Hills area. He joined the National Guard at the age of 14 to help bring money into his seven-person household. No one asked his age when he joined, so he continued, and was promoted to supply sergeant by the age of 16. He attended Officer Candidate School prior to the onset of World War II and was on active duty with the Intelligence and Reconnaissance (I&R) Platoon, Headquarters Company, 394th Infantry Regiment, attached to the 99th Infantry in World War II. At the tender age of 20, he was the second youngest in the unit and a lieutenant. Bouck led his platoon of 18 and four others in three separate battles near Lanzareth, Belgium, holding off over 500 Germans—official accounts say they were outnumbered 15 to 1—and thwarting German advancement for more than 12 hours. Nearly 100 Germans were killed. This was on December 16, 1944, the first morning of the Battle of the Bulge. The unit's gun barrels were so hot, it was later recalled, that they bent out of shape on the battlefield. Surrounded and outnumbered, Bouck and his men were captured and taken prisoner, serving time in several German stalags as prisoners of war. Lieutenant Bouck is seen at left during his service and below in 1981 as a retired captain. (Both photographs courtesy of SHHS.)

During their captivity, Lieutenant Bouck spent much time rallying his platoon members and encouraging them. Upon their release, all 18 members of Bouck's platoon were still alive. Bouck, however, too weak to file a report detailing what had happened, dismissed what they had done as part of war life. It was not until October 26, 1981, that Bouck and 14 members of their platoon received public recognition for their actions during the Battle of the Bulge. Secretary of the Army John O. Marsh Jr. hosted an awards ceremony in which all 18 members of Bouck's former platoon—or their survivors—were presented with Medals of Valor. The recognitions included the Presidential Unit Citation, four Distinguished Service Crosses—the second highest award for valor—five Silver Stars, and nine Stars with Valor Device. These awards made Bouck's one of the most highly decorated units in World War II. Above, from left to right, are Capt. Lyle Bouck, Secretary of the Army John Marsh, and Army chief of staff General Edward Meyer. Below, Captain Bouck is escorted while reviewing the troops at the 1981 ceremony. (Both photographs courtesy of SHHS.)

Capt. Bouck (right) thanks Commander of Troops Col. Don Phillips (left). Captain Bouck received the following awards for his actions near Lanzerath, Belgium in 1944: the Distinguished Service Cross, the Silver Star, the Bronze Star, the POW Medal, the Combat Infantryman Badge, the European-African-Middle-Eastern Campaign Medal with three Battle Stars, and three Purple Hearts: one medal and two oak leaf attachments. He also received the DAR Medal of Honor. The DAR also worked with the Lindbergh school district to bestow his high school diploma to him. Following World War II, Bouck returned to Sunset Hills, where he and his wife raised a family and he was a successful chiropractor. (Courtesy of SHHS.)

Gen. Edward Meyer, Army chief of staff, personally greets the members of the platoon being honored on October 26, 1981. They are, from left to right, General Meyer, Capt. Lyle Bouck, platoon member William Slape, platoon member Risto Milosevich, and Lucille James, the wife of a platoon member. John Eisenhower, ambassador to Belgium, was responsible for getting the entire platoon to Belgium. There, they sat with their former captors, and the German captors presented a medallion to Capt. Bouck. They remembered how he stood up for the men in his platoon and would not leave them. (Courtesy of SHHS.)

Through the efforts of brothers Bob and Pete Winter, bluebirds were able to be removed from the endangered species list. Those efforts also earned them a National DAR Conservation Award. (Courtesy of Bob and Wanda Winter.)

Father Justin Maurath (1921–1988) was a Catholic priest and military chaplain who served two tours of duty in Vietnam before 1968. So touched by the plight of the children he saw orphaned and alone, Father Just, as he was known, founded an orphanage there, under the direction of the Sisters of Saint Paul de Chartres. Father Maurath continued to use his family's residence on Eggeling Lane in Sunset Hills as his base until his death on January 11, 1988, of Agent Orange, cancer, and other complications. He is buried in Jefferson Barracks National Cemetery. Above, Maurath is pictured in his military uniform (left) and on the day of his ordination (right). Below, Father Justin is seen with several of the children from his orphanage. (All photographs courtesy of John Maurath.)

Sunset Hills resident Susan Bennet is a retired English teacher who was raised overseas in China and the Philippines. The author of three historical novels, Bennet gained her inspiration for the three books from the memoirs of her grandmother, Laura Walker. (Author's collection.)

Area resident Lynda S. Burch writes numerous children's musical e-books under her own name. Under the name of Lynda LaPorte, she also writes romantic suspense. She is the owner and publisher of Guardian Angel Publishing Inc. (GAP), which publishes award-winning children's literature. She also publishes an online, interactive, free monthly e-zine for kids for GAP. (Courtesy of Lynda S. Burch.)

Eileen Dreyer is a St. Louis native and a resident of Sunset Hills for over three decades. Her first career, as an area trauma nurse, provided fodder for her successful medical thrillers. She has been in publishing for over 25 years. She has published 38 books and eight short stories under both her name and as Kathleen Korbel. A *New York Times* best-selling, award-winning author in the genres of romance, paranormal, historical, and suspense, Dreyer is only the fourth person to be inducted into the Romance Writers of America Hall of Fame. (Courtesy of Eileen Dreyer.)

Local resident Jeannie Lin has been writing since she was a high school science teacher in South Central Los Angeles. In 2009, she was awarded that year's Golden Heart Award by Romance Writers of America for the best unpublished historical romance manuscript. She signed with Harlequin Mills & Boon. Her first two novels, *Butterfly Swords* and *The Dragon and the Pearl*, have created the Tang Dynasty historical romance subgenre for Harlequin Historical. (Courtesy of Jeannie Lin.)

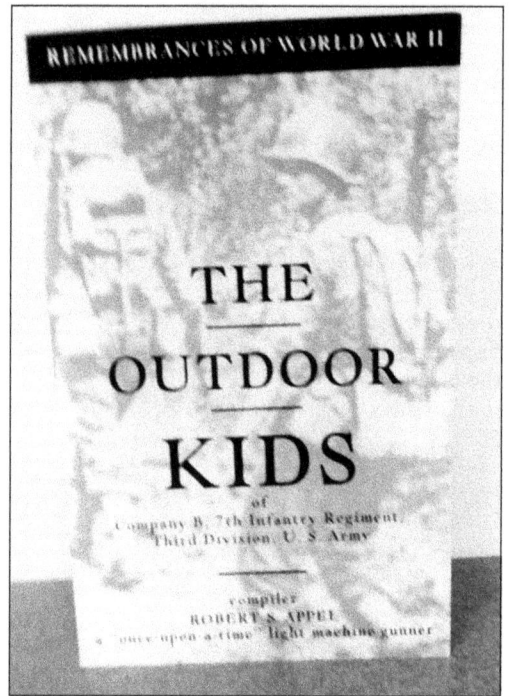

Various other authors from the area have published books, including Betty Burnett's *St. Louis at War*; Robert S. Appel's compilation of exploits of Company B, 7th Infantry, 3rd Division, *The Outdoor Kids*; Drum Hadley's book of poetry, *Voice of the Borderlands*; and Ed Thias's *Pencil Sketches of Missouri*. (All from author's collection.)

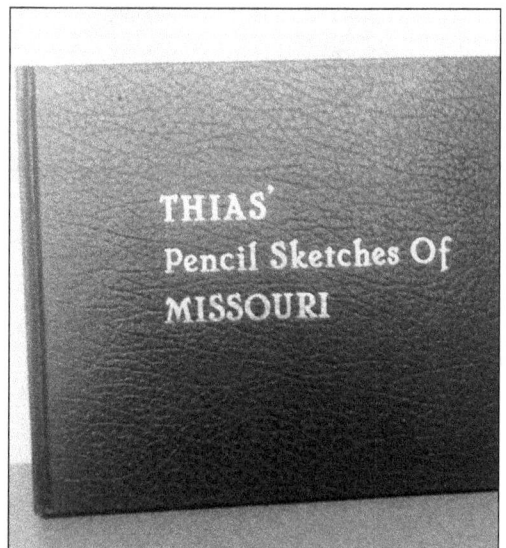

Eight

THE CITY OF SUNSET HILLS

CITY OF SUNSET HILLS NEWS LETTER

December, 1957 | Office Hours 9 - 3 Tuesdays & Fridays | Vol. I No. 1
10320 Hi-Way 66 | YO 6-4558

THE NEWSLETTER

An attempt will be made to mail this news letter, to be published periodically, to those listed on the personal property list, merchants, and others on license rolls.

BOARD WILL MEET MONDAY, DEC. 30

Because the regular meeting of the Board of Aldermen falls on the night of Dec. 24, it has been postponed until Monday, Dec. 30th. Regular meetings are held on the fourth Tuesday of each month at 8:00 P.M. at Rott School, Rott and Watson Roads.

LOCAL OPTION ELECTION SET

Action, taken at the Board's Nov. 26th meeting, followed the filing of petition by private individuals. Having found that petitions presented were sufficient, the Board of Aldermen of Sunset Hills ordered a special election for Jan. 3rd, 1958, on the question "shall intoxicating liquor containing alcohol in excess of five percent by weight, be sold by the drink at retail for consumption on the premises where sold."

The Board, through a statement issued by Robert Jones, special counsel to the Board, said the Aldermen "had no discretion but to go ahead and order the election, if the petition conformed to the Revised Missouri Statutes, Sec. 311.110."

He further stated that "in the event of a favorable vote to the proposition, the Board of Aldermen will still control and regulate by Ordinance the places serving liquor by the drink. "It should be noted that no one can serve liquor by the drink if the vote is favorable until Ordinance is passed by the Board of Aldermen setting up the qualifications for a license."

Polling Places

Lemay, 18 - New Mehlville Firehouse, Lindbergh & Sappington Bks. Rds.

Lemay, 20 - Thomas Jefferson School, Lindbergh and Robyn Rds.

Bonhomme, 14 - Art Britton Auction & Sales, 10315 Hi-Way 66.

Bonhomme, 15 - Rott School, Rott and Watson Rds.

SUNSET HILLS HIRES FULL TIME POLICEMAN

Board of Aldermen this week made arrangements to hire a policeman to patrol the City on a full time basis.

He is Donald Wagner of Overland. His duties will begin toward the end of December. The City is also making plans to purchase a three-way radio equipped car.

Residents will continue to call Parkview 7-8200 on police matters. This is the telephone number of the County Police Department. However, after the radio equipped car is in use, expected about the ... (cont. p. 2)

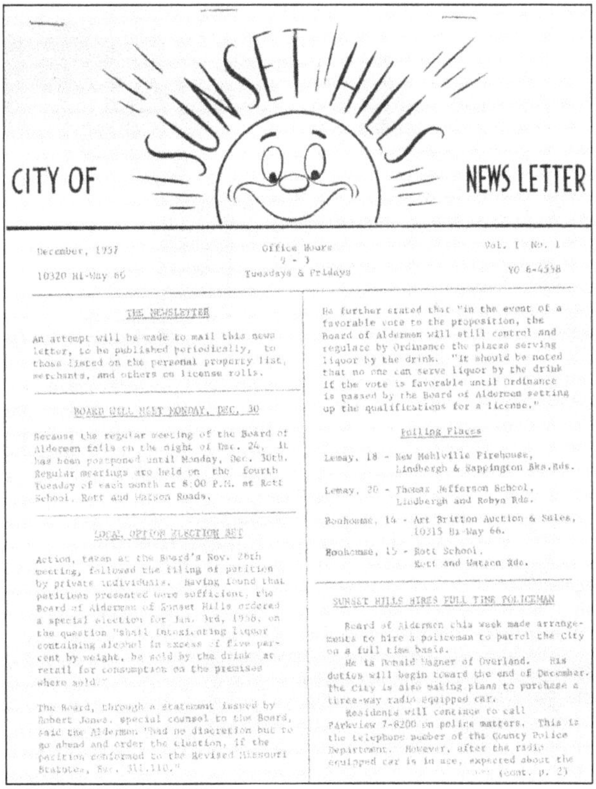

Sunset Hills filed a petition to incorporate as a city on May 22, 1954, and it was approved on June 5, 1957, by the St. Louis County Council. Kirkwood had filed suit prior to the incorporation to annex part of the area but the suit was withdrawn. The county council appointed three city officials and six aldermen to serve until the first municipal election could be held. It was scheduled for April 1958. Shown here is the first newsletter from the new city of Sunset Hills in 1957. (Courtesy of SHHS.)

Pictured are the front and back of the election brochure that was printed to familiarize the citizens of the new city with those running for office in the April 1958 election. (Both, courtesy of SHHS.)

A new city hall was built in 1980 along Lindbergh Boulevard. (Courtesy of SHHS.)

In 1973, the Sunset Hills Police Department was formed. This first department consisted of 10 officers and one civilian employee. The department has now grown to over 30, and has its own dispatch center. The new police department building was constructed in 1998. (Author's collection.)

The newest building on the complex is the Sunset Hills Community Center, which opened to the public in 2010. (Author's collection.)

The nonprofit Sunset Hills Historical Society was formed in 2004. Its office and archive are located in city hall. In 2007, the historical society helped the city celebrate its 50th anniversary by co-sponsoring many events. One of the society's charges has been to place granite markers in various historic Sunset Hills locations. The granite was salvaged from the Interstate 44 overpass when it was remodeled and one of the markers (above) was placed at Minnie HaHa Beach. The marker designates the site as a historic Indian landing and was dedicated in 2009. Below, Native American Silver Otter demonstrated his tools and crafts at the occasion. (Author's collection.)

Also present at the event was the 150-year-old, 36-star flag used to drape the casket of Confederate general Sterling Price (1809–1867). A veteran of the Mormon War, the Mexican War, and the Civil War, Price was pro-Union at first until the events of the Camp Jackson Affair swayed his loyalty toward the Confederate cause. He was also the governor of Missouri from 1853 to 1857. Glennon Franklin is shown holding the flag. (Above, author's collection; right, courtesy of LOC: LC-DIG-cwpb-07527.)

In 2007, the Sunset Hills Historical Society helped the city celebrate its 50th anniversary by co-sponsoring many events, including this car show. The show featured a wide range of vehicles, from the wooden delivery truck below to a fairy tale roadster. (Both, courtesy of SHHS.)

As part of the 50th anniversary celebration, Sunset Hills Historical Society sponsored a Veterans' Recognition evening on July 14, 2007. Hundreds showed up at the outdoor venue. The St. Louis 1950s band Sh-Boom performed, and active military and veterans from the area were honored for their service. (Courtesy of SHHS.)

One project that is dear to the Sunset Hills Historical Society involves giving quilts to local veterans, most of whom served in World War II. Monsignor Ed Griesedieck (left) and Alwal "Al" Anheuser Moore (below), who both fought in World War II, are among those who have received quilts. The Griesedieck and Anheuser families were among the early founding German immigrant families who settled in Sunset Hills in the late 1800s and early 1900s. (Both courtesy of Joyce Franklin.)

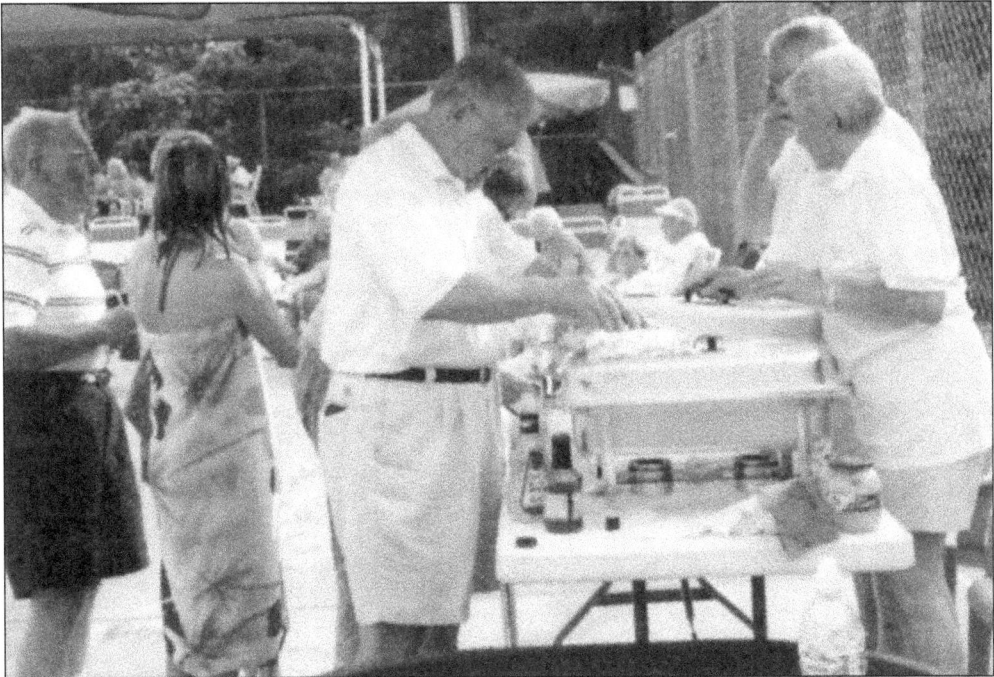

Sunset Hills Historical Society sponsors many annual events, including the German Fest. At the German Fest, attendees like Butch Thomas (center) dig in to some authentic German food. (Courtesy of SHHS.)

German dancers entertain the crowd at the German Fest. Many local families choose to have their children take classes promoting their German heritage and German arts. (Courtesy of SHHS.)

It would not be German Fest without a genuine German band and polka music. (Courtesy of SHHS.)

Accordions also add to the German flavor of the event. (Courtesy of SHHS.)

Nine

December 31, 2010

The morning of December 31, 2010, started like any other New Year's Eve, as people scurried around getting ready for their evening plans. No one expected the devastation that would occur just before noon. An EF3 (on the Enhanced Fujita Scale) tornado began its havoc in Murphy, Missouri, to the southwest of Sunset Hills in Jefferson County. According to the National Weather Service, a tornado touched down just east of Murphy at 11:48 a.m. with a damage path 40 yards wide. Jumping to the Jefferson–St. Louis County line, it was rated EF0 when it next touched down with a 50-yard-wide damage path. Traveling down Highway 30, the tornado next touched down at Saint Paul Catholic Church, pictured here, where it damaged the roof. (Courtesy of Judy Guglielemencci.)

Saint Paul's Elementary School, across the parking lot from the church, also sustained damage. Some windows in the school were blown out while others remained intact and a huge pile of tornado debris sat in front of the school. (Courtesy of Judy Guglielemencci.)

Behind the school, the tornado destroyed the parish rectory when it was rated an EF2 with a damage path of 100 yards. (Courtesy of Judy Guglielemencci.)

The tornado continued its path up the subdivision street adjacent to the church complex. As it traveled up the street, one huge branch punctured the roof of a split-level house. The branch landed on the ground floor, and its top protruded through the house's roof. As the tornado journeyed up to the top of Forest Knoll Drive, it passed through to Fenton City Park, crossing the Meramec River into Sunset Hills with the strength of an EF1. (Courtesy of Judy Guglielemencci.)

As the tornado crossed Interstate 270, it ran parallel with Old Watson Road. The tornado increased in strength and speed as it descended upon the heart of Sunset Hills at Lindbergh Boulevard at about 11:56 a.m. At this point, the tornado was rated between EF3 and high-level EF3. The damage path was determined to be a quarter of a mile. (Courtesy of City of Sunset Hills: Trish Moore.)

In Sunset Hills, the tornado hit various rows of trees, destroying some, while others remained untouched. (Photograph courtesy of City of Sunset Hills: Trish Moore.)

Tree limbs and utility lines merged and even the bark was stripped from the tops of some trees. (Courtesy of City of Sunset Hills: Trish Moore.)

The tornado pulled mature trees out of the ground by their roots. (Courtesy of City of Sunset Hills: Trish Moore.)

It also ripped entire squares of sod from the ground. (Courtesy of City of Sunset Hills: Trish Moore.)

On Lindbergh Boulevard and a strip mall parking lot fronting it, the tornado indiscriminately picked up two cars and turned them over, while leaving other cars alone. (Courtesy of City of Sunset Hills: Trish Moore.)

Two posts were rammed through the driver's side windshield of this parked car. (Courtesy of City of Sunset Hills: Trish Moore.)

The tornado ripped through Watson Trails Park, destroying shelters and playgrounds. (Courtesy of the City of Sunset Hills: Trish Moore.)

On Lindbergh Boulevard, one side of this bus stop was missing. (Courtesy of City of Sunset Hills: Trish Moore.)

With the loss of electricity, problems with the gas lines, and downed power lines, poles, and traffic standards, Lindbergh Boulevard was closed down for several days. (Courtesy of City of Sunset Hills: Trish Moore.)

In a strip mall on Lindbergh Boulevard, the unpredictable extent of the tornado is seen in the glass panes of this business. The pane on the door had been blown out, as had the third and fourth panes, while the middle remained intact. (Courtesy of City of Sunset Hills: Trish Moore.)

The actor John Goodman, part owner of a restaurant on Lindbergh Boulevard and a native of nearby Affton, came to examine the damage. (Courtesy of City of Sunset Hills: Trish Moore.)

The EF3 tornado tore the roofs off of some businesses and homes. (Courtesy of City of Sunset Hills: Trish Moore.)

In other areas, the damage was so severe it is impossible to tell what type of building the tornado destroyed. (Courtesy of City of Sunset Hills: Trish Moore.)

Buildings were damaged and then the twister picked up the debris and deposited it elsewhere. (Courtesy of City of Sunset Hills: Trish Moore.)

In other instances, the buildings seemed to just collapse onto themselves. (Courtesy of City of Sunset Hills: Trish Moore.)

Sometimes, it appeared the tornado hit from the side rather than from the top, as in this case, where one wall was blown out. (Courtesy of City of Sunset Hills: Trish Moore.)

In other cases, buildings and doors showed up far from where they belonged. (Courtesy of City of Sunset Hills: Trish Moore.)

Trees fell on cars in driveways. (Courtesy of City of Sunset Hills: Trish Moore.)

The intensity of the storm created balancing acts that defy understanding. (Courtesy of City of Sunset Hills: Trish Moore.)

Even adjacent to total destruction, some buildings and power lines were still standing. (Courtesy of Sunset Hills City Hall: Trish Moore.)

The cleanup began quickly. Some merchants were back in their stores as early as Tuesday, January 4. Many neighboring communities stepped up, sending equipment and manpower to help immediately.

Epilogue

In the aftermath of the tornado, the promise of a better new year seemed far away to the victims. But the kindness of the people in the area continues to manifest itself. Individual donations and various fundraisers held by businesses, schools, churches, and other organizations have raised more than $250,000, all of which has gone straight to the victims of the tornado. Debbie Loeffelman, owner of Johnny's Market, merely placed a container at the end of each register, and managed to collect $2,000. Coming together is not hard to do in this community full of people with deep roots, strong beliefs, and good hearts.

Visit us at
arcadiapublishing.com

www.ingramcontent.com/pod-product-compliance
Lightning Source LLC
Chambersburg PA
CBHW050559110426
42813CB00008B/2407